This book is dedicated to all who cherish

America's history as a vast heritage of people and events—some

heroic, some inglorious, but all part of America's epic struggle

to come of age—and to all who know that understanding

the past is essential to dealing with the present.

NATIONAL PARKS
of WASHINGTON D.C.

THE STORY BEHIND THE SCENERY®

by Robert Fudge

ROBERT FUDGE is the Chief of Interpretation and Education for the National Park Service Northeast Region. He lived and worked in Washington, DC, and formerly served as the Deputy Chief of Visitor Services for the National Mall & Memorial Parks.

The National Parks of Washington, DC *include some of America's oldest federal parklands – monuments and memorials, parkways, historic sites, and natural areas in Virginia, Maryland, and the District of Columbia.*

Front Cover: Spring's Cherry Blossoms Frame the Washington Monument. Inside Cover: A Poetic Boulder Bridge Over Rock Creek in Spring. Photos by Eric Long. Title Page: American Flags Wave Proudly in Front of the Washington Monument. Photo by Laurence Parent. Page 2/3: The Steps of the Lincoln Memorial. Photo by Eric Long.

Edited by Maryellen Conner • Book design by K. C. DenDooven.

Second Printing, 2009

NATIONAL PARKS OF WASHINGTON D.C.: THE STORY BEHIND THE SCENERY © 2006 KC PUBLICATIONS, INC.
"The Story Behind the Scenery"; the Eagle / Flag icon on Front Cover are registered in the U.S. Patent and Trademark Office.
LC 2006925546. ISBN 978-0-88714-266-6.

*The monuments and memorials in Washington, DC
are more than metal and stone. For generations they have
served as manifestations of achievements, hopes and dreams.*

These sites are considered sacred not just because of their appearance, but also because they continue to inspire with their timeless relevance.

The National Parks of Washington DC

Wherever people go in Washington DC, they are not far from a National Park area. Woodlands, meadows and cascading waters stretch into the very heart of the city. Gleaming monuments and memorials accent the landscape. Inviting gardens, statues, and fountains grace public spaces, and numerous historic sites recall the perseverance and accomplishments of previous generations. The National Parks of the Nation's capital represent a remarkable array of places, some famous, others virtually unknown, all with a treasure trove of stories, giving expression to American values. Together they provide a blend of natural and cultural history unsurpassed by any other American city. They are places of enduring meaning that are linked to one another, and to the hearts of the American people.

ERIC LONG

The White House is the oldest public building in Washington, DC. Although under the care of the National Park Service, President's Park is no ordinary national park. Here rangers, curators and maintenance workers must daily work around presidential events, activities and functions, while maintaining the lawns and gardens, preserving historic furnishings, and coordinating services for the visiting public.

"A century hence if this country keeps united... will produce a city, though not so large as London, yet of a magnitude inferi- or to few others in Europe, on the banks of the Potomac..."
—GEORGE WASHINGTON

ERIC LONG

Kite enthusiasts flock to the National Mall each year as part of the Smithsonian Institution's Kite Festival. Here spectacular displays of color, creativity and ingenuity take flight. The expanse of the National Mall is used extensively as a gathering spot for public events, celebrations and demonstrations - an ideal setting for free expression.

ANNE TUBIOLO

There is much in a name at the Vietnam Veterans Memorial. Each one engraved represents a person who gave their life in service to their country. On request, park rangers and volunteers will make rubbings of these names, giving them to those who wish to remember and honor a veteran.

*This confluence has always
been a natural meeting place for people.
Algonquian Indians pulled up their dugout
canoes, and constructed their villages here.*

On the Banks of the Potomac

MARK GIBSON

People have long associated Washington, DC with the Potomac River. It is as much a part of the capital's landscape as the Washington Monument. The Potomac is in essence the oldest feature of the city, and one that played a formidable part in Washington's history. Today it is surrounded by parkland, much of which recalls an earlier time, long before there was a republic, when nature ruled the landscape.

THE FIRST INHABITANTS

Just south of the cataracts of Great Falls and the narrows of Mather Gorge is the junction of the Potomac and Anacostia Rivers. This confluence has always been a natural meeting place for people. Thousands of years before Europeans built streets and structures near the riverbanks, Algonquian Indians pulled up their dugout canoes, and constructed their villages here. No less than three large Native American settlements are known to have existed where these two rivers meet. The clear waters were abundant with shad, perch, sturgeon, catfish, rockfish and herring. By the banks were birds by the millions, woodland buffalo, beaver, bear, fox, elk, and deer. For these early inhabitants, who hunted

Standing at a park overlook, onlookers can marvel at roaring waterfalls and churning eddies. Great Falls, on the Potomac River, is only a few miles from the center of the capital. This truly great natural setting has remained relatively unchanged since the days when Algonquian Indians fished in its waters.

In the 1820s Isaac Peirce and his stone-mason son Abner built a mill on Rock Creek. This handsome structure was erected at a time when early Americans ground their grain into flour at gristmills. When the waterwheel at Peirce Mill turns, an array of gears, belts, sifters and large grinding stones come to life. Waterpower opened the way for industry and made people like Isaac Peirce indispensable to their communities.

and fished, the Potomac and the Anacostia Rivers were a veritable source of life.

Archeologists have uncovered Native American quarries along Rock Creek, a Potomac tributary, as well as various encampments and settlements along the riverbanks. The largest of the known Indian villages was Nacotchtank, located on the southeast banks of the Anacostia. These agricultural people lived by the river for over 10,000 years. In 1608 it was the Nacotchtanks who greeted European explorer Captain John Smith. Only a few years later, a steady stream of Europeans followed. The Nacotchtanks traded and sometimes fought with these new arrivals. The relentless onslaught of settlers, and the European diseases that accompanied them, had a devastating effect on their number. Many died, others left to find refuge in lands to the west, and some stayed, adopting the ways of another culture. By 1660 Nacotchtank was no more.

A Capital Is Born

The river environment began to change and its banks bustled with new activities. By the mid 18th century the colonial port towns of Alexandria, Virginia, and Georgetown, Maryland were established. Farmers brought in their livestock and crops, sailing vessels arrived daily with supplies, and often slave

ships came in to port to sell their human cargo. The bustling towns witnessed a rising middle class of merchants and farmers. This confluence of rivers became a meeting place of cultures. It was still a frontier backwater, but its location at the conjunction of two rivers, and as the last port on the Potomac, from which a ship could sail to the Chesapeake Bay, made it a natural place for colonial commerce and industry.

By 1790 the infant nation had ratified the U.S. Constitution, and through a unanimous vote of the Electoral College had chosen George Washington to be the First President. However, there was still no permanent capital. Congress convened in New York and later Philadelphia. Representatives quarreled regularly about where the permanent seat of government should be. Some wanted it in the south; others wanted it in the north. An even more contentious issue facing the Congress at the time was how to pay off the national debt that was crippling the Nation. Some states felt they had already paid their fair share and were against further payment through taxation. Secretary of the Treasury Alexander Hamilton and Secretary of State Thomas Jefferson engineered a compromise whereby the permanent capital would be established in the south on the banks of the Potomac River in exchange for crucial

The massive U.S. Capitol dome, the soaring Washington Monument, and the colonnaded Lincoln Memorial create a majestic night scene. Pierre Charles L'Enfant's vision of a great capital by the Potomac River was realized, but today Washington, DC remains a work in progress - a city that strives to respond to the will and the needs of the people of the United States, and to whatever history may bring.

southern votes to support the debt tax. The compromise worked and in July of 1790 Congress authorized the new seat of government to be situated near the Potomac and the Anacostia Rivers. Three commissioners were appointed by President Washington to "define and limit a district of territory" which would occupy a federal district of a 10 mile square area to be ceded by the states of Virginia and Maryland.

The capital of the new republic would rise from an area of marshes, rolling hills, pastures, woodlots and meandering creeks. To survey the land, plan the city, and establish the territory to be ceded, President Washington in 1791 appointed two highly respected former military men, both 37 years of age: mild mannered Major Andrew Ellicott, arguably the foremost surveyor of his day, and the accomplished impetuous French architect and military engineer, Major Pierre Charles L'Enfant. L'Enfant would superintend the survey and design the streets and public spaces of the city. Ellicott would map the territory, plot the streets, and determine the boundaries. Accompanying Major Ellicott was his assistant, 60-year-old Benjamin Banneker. Banneker was a brilliant mathematician and an enlightened man of science. He was also an African American and former slave. Using surveying and astronomical equipment, he would make the calculations that would assure the survey's accuracy, and further define the boundaries of the diamond-shaped district. It was a dissimilar group, but a remarkable team. Their work would have far reaching implications for the capital.

PLANNING THE CITY

["L'Enfant] brought elements of the natural landscape into the heart of the city. In doing so he combined garden and urban design in a civic composition of enormous scale, great complexity, and almost bewildering variety."

JOHN W. REPS

As President Washington's Secretary of State, Thomas Jefferson also brought his influence and artistic sensibilities to bear. He corresponded frequently with Major L'Enfant, and provided him city plans collected from his travels in Europe. But the interest and influence of Jefferson and Washington not withstanding, L'Enfant had his own ideas, and soon prevailed upon the President to stretch his vision for the city. His idealistic plan called for vast public spaces and sweeping majestic avenues. He described a great city of 800,000, a palace for the President, a magnificent capitol building, ceremonial fountains, monuments, and a grand canal. To some L'Enfant's vision was audacious, but to Washington, it was inspired.

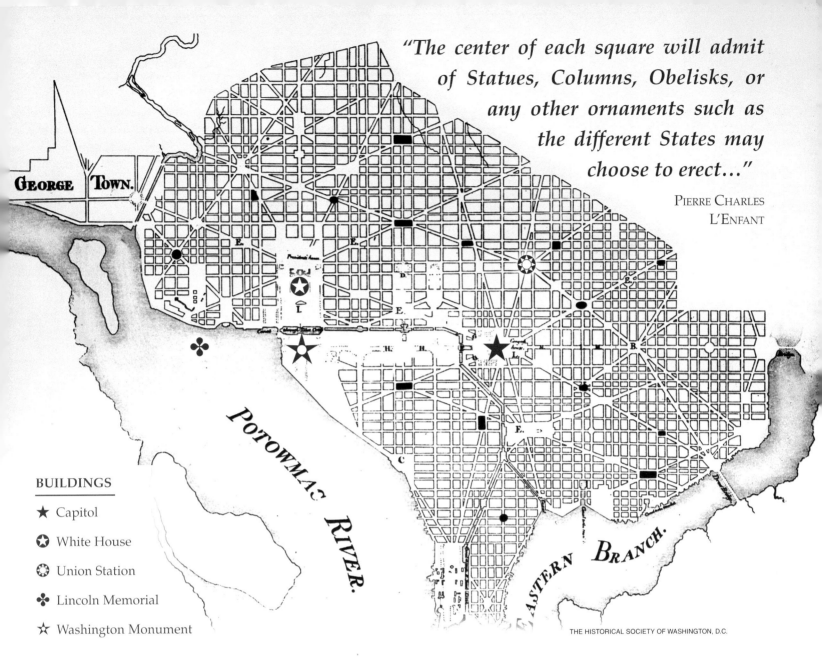

"The center of each square will admit of Statues, Columns, Obelisks, or any other ornaments such as the different States may choose to erect..."

PIERRE CHARLES
L'ENFANT

BUILDINGS

★ Capitol

✪ White House

✵ Union Station

♣ Lincoln Memorial

☆ Washington Monument

ERIC LONG

In 1792, in letters, Pierre L'Enfant gushed to President Washington that his design for the Capital would be the envy of the world. He described radiating avenues, grand spaces, formidable public buildings and places of honor for great Americans. The suggestion that areas be reserved to honor extraordinary citizens was a departure from conventions of his day. In great capitals elsewhere statues and parks had been reserved for nobility. L'Enfant realized the new republic should model something democratic and inspirational. Today, Washington, DC reflects what he envisioned, not only his ambitious design for public spaces, but also his articulated desire to provide for places that would "invite the youths of succeeding generations to tread in the paths of ...sages..."

Pierre L'Enfant died in 1825. He was buried on a farm in Maryland. In 1909 his remains were disinterred by a special act of Congress. He was laid in state in the U.S. Capitol and reburied in Arlington National Cemetery. His marble tablet displays his plan for the capital and reads "...ENGINEER-ARTIST-SOLDIER..."

The Old Stone House located in Georgetown is a simple 18th century structure and is considered the oldest building in the city. This unassuming dwelling would have been typical of many found in towns along the Potomac River. Georgetown, formerly part of Maryland, predates Washington, DC. In 1791 the town's newspaper announced the arrival of two newcomers, one "a gentleman of superior astronomical abilities," and the other a "French gentleman employed by the President of the United States." Indeed it was big news, Andrew Ellicott and Pierre L'Enfant had arrived to fashion the new Capital of the United States.

ERIC LONG

THE TEMPERAMENTAL VISIONARY

Major L'Enfant soon began to alienate himself from the commissioners assigned to monitor his progress. He deliberately ignored them and chose to communicate only to the President. Although Washington remained faithful to L'Enfant and gave him creative freedom, he became increasingly concerned by his volatile nature and inability to follow instructions.

Problems reached a peak when a local landowner, Daniel Carroll, began constructing a house on land that L'Enfant had reserved for one of the city's main thoroughfares. L'Enfant demanded that the house be removed. When Carroll refused, the furious Frenchman ordered his workmen to demolish it, which they did. Washington admonished the headstrong architect and directed him not to touch private property again. In addition, he ordered him

to take his instructions directly from the commissioners. When L'Enfant balked at the imposed conditions, the President had him dismissed.

With the removal of the tempestuous L'Enfant in 1792, Ellicott became the principal planner of the city. L'Enfant refused to provide his former assistant with any of his drawings. Ellicott was left to reconstruct the plan from his personal notes and memory. When the city plan was finally printed and distributed, L'Enfant's name was absent from the engraving; but most of his ideas for the city remained unchanged and intact.

In 1814 L'Enfant once again was called on, this time by Secretary of War James Monroe who commissioned him to reconstruct defenses south of the capital on the Potomac River. Acrimony once again

The C&O Canal had 74 locks. One of the most formidable lock houses was Great Falls Tavern. It was the home of the lockkeeper and offered weary travelers food and lodging. The railroads, and a series of devastating floods, put an end to canal commerce. Today the old towpath is preserved as a National Historical Park.

In 1828 a great "national project" was launched to create a 460-mile-long canal that would stretch from Georgetown to the Ohio River. It took 22 years to build a roughly 185-mile portion, but The Chesapeake and Ohio Canal never quite reached its intended destination. Heavily laden barges pulled by mules on towpaths brought goods, passengers and supplies upriver. Lumber, grains and coal were transported downriver.

ERIC LONG

led to the architect's dismissal after he refused to comply fully with the Secretary's orders. In the years that followed, L'Enfant languished into obscurity. When he died he was buried in a pauper's grave. In 1909, with great ceremony, his remains were removed and re-interred in Arlington National Cemetery. The irascible visionary was finally recognized for his contributions.

A Capital Image

"…The most luminous point of American territory; a city recently transformed and made beautiful in its body and in its spirit."

FREDERICK DOUGLASS

Magnificent Intentions

Washington, DC's transformation to become a world-class city began in fits and starts, and at times seemed almost doomed to failure. The city started with a terrain of pastures, shacks and marshes. L'Enfant's ideas, on paper, impressed speculators. Construction workers arrived in a steady stream. Formidable buildings began to go up along the land that had been cleared for streets. In this sparsely populated hamlet, grand avenues along with rising and imposing marble structures seemed out of place. However, a persistent optimism prevailed; and with the arrival of the federal government in 1800, the idea of a permanent capital for the United States had evolved into a reality.

The Mall was a pasture, the ceremonial canal was a languid creek, and Pennsylvania Avenue was

ERIC LONG

On the Mall stands the oldest Smithsonian museum, "the Castle." Here during the Victorian era visitors toured the gardens and marveled at scientific "curiosities." The National Park Service does not operate the Smithsonian Institution, but it often cooperates with it as a sister agency dedicated to education and conservation.

alternately mud and dust. L'Enfant's ambitious plan of fountains, monuments, and gardens was still just an idea. For some visitors the capital of the republic was a grand disappointment. In 1840 one such ungracious assessment by a visitor described it as " a deserted village in an unwholesome country...the most forlorn and melancholy place, bearing the name of capital I ever was in..." In 1842 the British author Charles Dickens visited the city and wrote with biting sarcasm, "the City of Magnificent Distances [is in reality] the City of Magnificent Intentions...[it contains]...spacious avenues, that begin in nothing, and lead nowhere..."

AN APPEARANCE OF OPTIMISM

Still Washington, DC grew. A railroad station was constructed on the Mall. Feedlots, lumberyards and foundries were in abundance. Additional workers arrived daily: most were slaves, free blacks, new immigrants from Europe, and the Nation's poor. In the midst of so much industry there were still attempts at beauty and culture. The Smithsonian Institution's first building was erected on the Mall. "The Castle," as it was called, with its collection of national treasures, was the result of a bequest in 1829 by an English scientist, James Smithson. Smithson had never visited the United States but willed his fortune to Americans to promote "knowledge among men."

Later in 1850 the landscape architect Andrew Jackson Downing began planning gardens for the Mall. Downing stated that one of his main objectives was to "form a National Park, which should be

Subsistence farmers populated much of northeast Virginia before the American Revolution. Claude Moore Colonial Farm at Turkey Run recalls those early days of hardship and hope. The National Park Service formerly operated the living history farm. Today it is still part of the National Park System, but run by the Friends of Claude Moore Colonial Farm at Turkey Run.

MARK GIBSON

ERIC LONG

In Oxon Cove Park is Oxon Hill Farm. The farm was once part of Saint Elizabeth's Hospital and was operated by the hospital's patients. Its pastoral surroundings are still therapeutic, but it is better known today as a place for school programs, farming demonstrations and special events.

an ornament to the Capital of the United States." The Downing Plan, with its serpentine pathways and abundant plantings was modeled from cemeteries, which in Downing's day were fashionable as places to stroll and picnic. L'Enfant's open lawn was gradually becoming something resembling a 19th century cemetery.

In the 1860s, during the Civil War, Washington, DC became one vast military encampment. Parks and monuments were neglected. Gardens and open spaces were trampled. Livestock was penned in public areas, and troops paraded and drilled daily on streets and on the Mall. A military presence was evident throughout the city and L'Enfant's "ceremonial canal" served as an open sewer.

Suggested Readings

LEVEY, BOB AND JANE, *Washington Album: A Pictorial History of the Nation's Capital*, The Washington Post Books, 2000.

REPS, JOHN W., *Washington on View: The Nation's Capital Since 1790,* The University of North Carolina Press, 1991.

In 1930 the George Washington Memorial Parkway was authorized. Soon new parks were transforming Washington. It became one of the most attractive cities in the world.

Creating National Parks in Washington D.C.

ERIC LONG

After the Civil War ended, the Nation became pre-occupied with national reconstruction, but the reconstruction of gardens and parks was not a priority. The Nation's Centennial came and went with relative little thought given to Washington's appearance. However, the reunited states needed symbols to rally around, and people were hungry for the peace and repose that parks could bring to their battered lives.

PARKS FOR THE PEOPLE

By the turn of the century new statues were added to squares and triangles. Public gardens were everywhere. In 1890 Rock Creek Park, the first federal park, was established "...for the benefit and enjoyment of the people of the United States." The park movement was in full swing in 1901 when the McMillan Commission, named after the commission's chairman Senator James McMillan, revived many of the concepts in the L'Enfant Plan. Their new designs called for draining marshes and dumping dredged river sediments into retaining sea walls to create more than 700 acres of park land west and south of the Washington Monument.

A grand monument to President Lincoln with a reflecting pool was to be constructed at the terminus of this new land.

One of America's older National Parks, Rock Creek *Park is only minutes away from city streets. During weekends, sections of the parkway are closed to motorized vehicles, offering bikers and hikers outstanding opportunities to take in eye-catching scenery at a slower pace.*

- 14 -

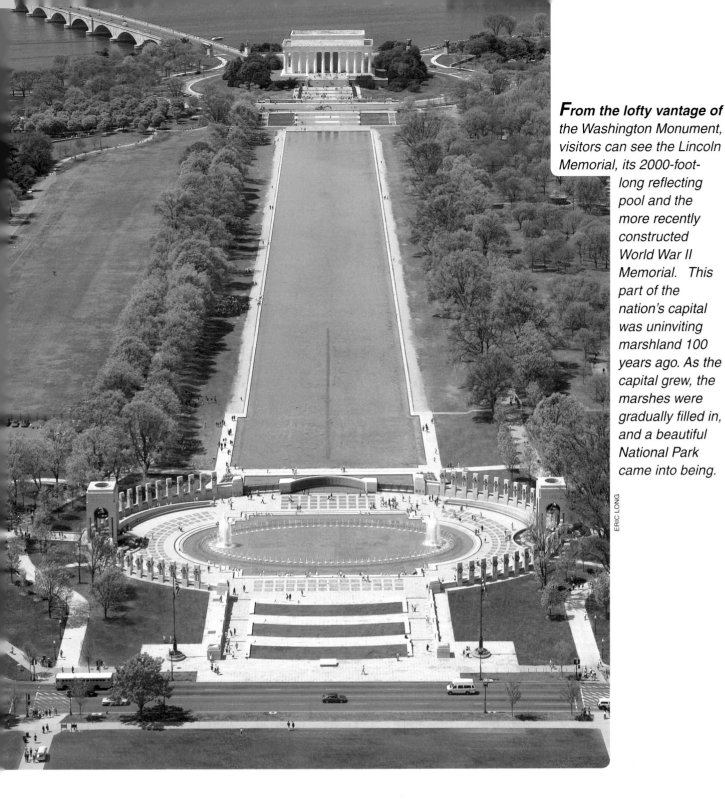

From the lofty vantage of the Washington Monument, visitors can see the Lincoln Memorial, its 2000-foot-long reflecting pool and the more recently constructed World War II Memorial. This part of the nation's capital was uninviting marshland 100 years ago. As the capital grew, the marshes were gradually filled in, and a beautiful National Park came into being.

ERIC LONG

Reclaiming the marshes of the Anacostia for public parks was called for, and the meandering forest road following the picturesque Rock Creek was to become a federally protected scenic carriage route. President Theodore Roosevelt was a great advocate for the outdoors and delighted in riding horseback through the capital's nearby parks. The athletic and unabashed "TR" was known to skinny-dip on occasion in Rock Creek.

A Blossoming Idea

In the early 1900s various Washington garden enthusiasts began to plant Japanese flowering cherry trees in surrounding neighborhoods. First Lady Helen Taft, who had once lived in Japan, had long admired these ornamental trees. She enthusiastically extended her support to the idea of planting them along the avenues of the city. Dr. Jokichi Takamine, a world-renowned chemist from Tokyo, heard about the citizens' effort to plant the trees. While in Washington he visited the President, and in the company of Japanese officials generously offered to personally donate 2,000 trees in the name of his native city.

When they arrived in 1910, after their long journey across the Pacific, the Department of Agriculture determined they were infested with insects and disease. President Taft ordered them burned. What

Water cascades over the dam at Peirce
Mill in Rock Creek Park. Much was saved in
1890 when Congress set aside this land
to be a federal park.

had begun as an honorable act of friendship had all the trappings of an international incident. Dr. Takamine resolved the sensitive situation by offering to replace the infested trees.

In 1912 the second shipment of 3,020 trees arrived. Most were Yoshino cherries, but 11 other species were included. First Lady Helen Taft and the Viscountess Chinda, wife of the Japanese Ambassador, participated in a tree planting ceremony to celebrate the new arrivals. As years passed more trees were planted and propagated. Today over 3,700 flowering cherry trees of various species, some over 50 feet tall, adorn the city's monumental core. Together they remain a cherished living symbol of international friendship; and for a few awe-inspiring spring days, they become the city's greatest attraction.

A Green Oasis

With the advent of the automobile many more Americans engaged in recreational travel. The newly formed National Capital Park and Planning Commission capitalized on the potential of roadways to bring people to the parks. Park planners revisited the L'Enfant and McMillan Commission plans and recommended new parklands and parkways.

Rock Creek Park was extended to provide for a longer scenic drive, and in 1930 the George Washington Memorial Parkway was authorized. Architects, with attention to bucolic and artistic esthetics, designed arched bridges of stone to span roadways, streams and rivers. Anacostia Park was extended northward, and new recreational facilities were constructed along the Potomac. Cricket, hockey, and polo fields, picnic groves, tennis courts, golf courses, bridle paths, nature trails, and even a campground were added in the city.

Soon new parks were transforming Washington. In stark contrast to its past, it became one of the most attractive cities in the world. After the transference of federal city parks and monuments from the Office of Public Buildings and Parks to the National Park Service in 1934, Washington became a green oasis, managed with special attention to preservation, conservation, and recreation.

Even as the Great Depression gripped the Nation, armies of young men under the Civilian Conservation Corps worked to establish parks and recreational areas in the District; and, in spite of segregation, the needs of black residents were being accommodated with the construction of "Colored" golf courses, swimming pools and playing fields. During the second half of the 20th century, citizen efforts to preserve historic homes, public squares, statues, and even a former amusement park, proved successful. Washington, DC was quickly becoming more than just an attraction; it was becoming a more livable city.

Suggested Reading

Bednar, Michael, *L'Enfant's Legacy: Public Open Spaces in Washington, D.C.*, The John Hopkins University Press, 2006.

In spring Japanese cherry trees provide a breathtaking backdrop for the city's monuments and memorials. In April of 1999 a beaver appeared in the Tidal Basin. Cherry trees in bloom were chewed down. The surprising news spread worldwide. After a few hair-raising days rangers caught and unceremoniously relocated the furry troublemaker.

Actor John Wilkes Booth was reading his mail that morning on the steps of Ford's Theatre when the First Lady's messenger arrived to reserve seats for the presidential party.

Wars Come to Washington

For over two centuries America endured a series of wars, and people looked to the capital as a place to recognize the courage, sacrifice and service to country of those who fought. Today not only do statues, monuments and memorials recall conflicts of the past, so do the remains of earthworks, forts, military artifacts and structures. War has been very immediate and real to Washington, DC, and even bloodshed and destruction have found their way into the capital.

THE BURNING OF THE CAPITAL

On August 24, 1814 in Bladensburg, Maryland, just east of the federal city, American forces were routed by British troops under the command of Major General Robert Ross. The victorious General Ross ordered his men to march on Washington. It was the lowest point of the War of 1812 for the Americans. The government, the American army, and many of the city's terrified inhabitants, fled. In an attempt to deny the invaders military stores, Americans set fire to their arsenals and the city's navy yard.

ERIC LONG

In the summer of 1814 invading British soldiers *destroyed the new nation's capital. Months later General Andrew Jackson repelled the British at the Battle of New Orleans. Jackson was later elected President. In 1853 an equestrian statue was erected in Lafayette Square in his honor. It faces the White House and depicts the jaunty Jackson tipping his hat.*

New defenses were erected shortly after the British attack on the capital. The most impressive was Fort Washington. It was strategically located south of the city on a bluff overlooking the Potomac. An awesome sight, it had numerous cannons, massive brick walls, a moat and a drawbridge. The fort continued to change with the times. Concrete batteries were constructed for rapid-fire guns, and larger and larger artillery took the place of cannons. In 1946 the old fort was determined to be obsolete, and subsequently it was transferred to the Interior Department. Today lofty parapets provide historic insights into times of war and peace, and give park visitors spectacular views of the surrounding countryside.

ERIC LONG

With enemy troops already marching in the streets, the President's wife, Dolley Madison, along with clerks, slaves, and a handful of Washington citizens, spirited away and saved the Declaration of Independence, White House valuables, and a full-length portrait of George Washington painted by Gilbert Stuart.

General Ross received little resistance as he marched his troops down the city's deserted streets. The White House, the U.S. Capitol, and other government structures were left undefended. Ross ordered his men to burn only public buildings; however, several private homes were also torched.

As the U.S. Capitol, the White House, the Navy Yard, military stores and abandoned ships at dock burned, a thunderstorm brewed. Torrential rains stopped some of the fires, but the following day the British resumed their campaign of destruction. Still the storms persisted with gale force winds. In the midst of it all, a catastrophic gunpowder explosion killed 30 British soldiers. The British, believing they had broken the back of the new American government, left the foreboding city and marched back to their ships and sailed toward Baltimore. General Ross would be killed in action weeks later near Baltimore, but the city of Washington would rebound, as Americans returned to raise hope from the ashes of the Nation's capital.

FORTIFYING WASHINGTON

After the retreat of the Union army in the First Battle of Manassas in 1861, hysteria spread through the streets of Washington as many feared the city would be overtaken by Confederate forces. In a matter of days scores of forts were hastily erected to circle the capital city, most on private property. Many watched as their farms and gardens were eliminated to make way for barracks, earthworks, stockades, and gun emplacements.

Toward the end of the Civil War the city was indeed attacked. Confederate Lieutenant General Jubal Early had just defeated Union troops at Monocacy near Frederick, Maryland. On July 11, 1864 his forces arrived in sight of the U.S. Capitol with its newly finished dome. Only Fort Stevens stood between him and the city. Once again, people were in a panic as word spread that the city was under attack. Reinforcements were on their way but had not yet arrived. The garrison was ill prepared for the impending assault. All available were manning the defenses, including clerks, and veterans who had been convalescing at a nearby hospital.

In July of 1864 Confederate troops attacked Washington. At Monocacy they met their first resistance. Today rock walls and fences mark the battlefield where Confederate forces were victorious but delayed, giving the Union army time to reinforce the capital's defenses.

As Confederate troops approached, the Union soldiers opened fire with heavy artillery. General Early hesitated in launching an all out assault. As time passed, reinforcements arrived and even the President and Mrs. Lincoln came to assess the situation. Confederate bullets whistled past the President's ears as he peered over the garrison walls. That evening a large contingent of Union forces sent by General Grant arrived and converged on the scene. The next day General Early realized attacking would be futile. He withdrew and headed for the Shenandoah Valley.

A GHASTLY ACT

On April 14, 1865 people in Washington, DC were still celebrating in the streets, having heard that the Army of Northern Virginia under General Robert E. Lee had surrendered to General Grant and Union forces at the village of Appomattox Court House. A complete Union victory seemed imminent. That day President Lincoln spent time with his oldest son, Robert, who was home on leave after serving with General Grant. Later in the day Lincoln would meet with his Cabinet to begin planning for the reconstruction of the South. In the afternoon he took a leisurely carriage ride with his wife. They had plans to attend a play at Ford's Theatre later that evening.

Actor John Wilkes Booth was reading his mail that morning on the steps of Ford's Theatre when the First Lady's messenger arrived to reserve seats for the presidential party. Booth maintained a secret life as a supporter of the Southern cause, and had previously conspired to kidnap the President.

Lee's surrender made Booth believe that nothing short of the overthrow of the government would change the course of impending events. He saw his opportunity when he heard that the President and Mrs. Lincoln would be attending the theater. He set an assassination plan in motion and hurriedly plotted, not only to kill the President, but also to use accomplices to kill Vice President Andrew Johnson, and Secretary of State William Henry Seward. Although the Secretary of State was attacked and severely injured, the accomplices murdered no one; but their tenacious leader followed his self appointed task with a deadly precision.

The presidential party arrived at Ford's Theatre that night, and took their seats in the State Box decorated with flags. The play was a comedy entitled "Our American Cousin." As the presidential party laughed through comic scenes, Booth slipped into a hallway behind where they were seated. Actor Harry Hawk was on stage playing the fool and had just delivered a hilarious insult, when Booth stepped out, aimed his Derringer, and shot the President in the back of the head. Major Henry Rathbone, one of President's guests in the State Box, jumped up and tried to subdue the assassin. Booth lunged and severely wounded the Major with a large dagger he was wielding.

The "state box" where President and Mrs. Lincoln sat on Friday, April 14th, 1865 is draped in flags as it was that night. Many details have been restored, from the hanging portrait of President George Washington to the crimson damask sofas. Today performances once again enliven the theater, but the decorated state box remains empty, a memorial to the man who "saved the Union" and advanced the cause of freedom.

On 10th Street across from Ford's Theatre is the Petersen House. Mortally wounded, Lincoln was carried there and placed in a bed rented by a boarder. The street outside filled as news spread that the President was shot. Doctors, officials and family members rushed to the scene. At 7:22 a.m. on April 15th the agonizing wait was over. Abraham Lincoln was dead.

"...the Declaration of Independence gave liberty, not alone to the people of this country, but I hope, to the world, for all future time...I would rather be assassinated on this spot than surrender it."

—ABRAHAM LINCOLN
FEBRUARY 22, 1861

PHOTOS BY ANNE TUBIOLO

A solemn atmosphere prevails at the Tomb of the Unknowns in Arlington National Cemetery. Buried here are unidentified American soldiers from World War I, World War II and the Korean War. This site is a center for Veterans Day and Memorial Day events. Although not a National Park, Arlington National Cemetery is in every sense a memorial.

Screams and shouts were quickly replacing laughter in the theater. Then Booth leaped to the stage floor. Waving his bloody dagger he shouted, "Sic semper tyrannis!" - a Latin phrase he had used as a Shakespearian actor, meaning, "thus always to tyrants." With many in the audience still in shock, he ran off stage, out of the theater, and away on a horse. Soldiers and doctors transported President Lincoln across the street from the theater to a room in a boarding house. The President never regained consciousness and passed away the next morning on April 15th on a bed too small for his tall frame.

For days Booth remained a fugitive until he was found hiding in a barn in southern Maryland. There he was fatally shot by one of his pursuers. Booth's ghastly act had dashed the best hopes for the country. President Lincoln had beseeched Americans to "bind up the Nation's wounds." His murder inspired calls for retribution against the South. It would take much longer for the healing to begin.

HONORING SERVICE TO COUNTRY

At the end of the 19th century American servicemen were called into action again, first in the Spanish-American War and then with the Philippine-American War. Many died from battle, and many more died from disease. In spite of the casualties and with the exception of gravesites and monuments in Arlington National Cemetery, there was little done in the capital to reflect their service to country. As the presidential monuments to Washington and Lincoln were completed, and statues were erected to generals and admirals, memorials to the contributions of common soldiers remained relatively obscure. In 1931, in the midst of the Great Depression, the first memorial to veterans was erected on the National Mall. For today's visitors it can be easily overlooked, south of the Lincoln Memorial Reflecting Pool. The DC War Memorial was erected as a civic initiative by Washingtonians who wanted to recognize city

The Vietnam Veterans Memorial is often known as "the Wall." Over 58,000 souls are chronicled here. Drawn to its vortex, onlookers find themselves surrounded by the solemnity of glistening black granite. They can be transfixed by names of the fallen, appearing as if engraved over their own reflections – present and past, living and lost, mingled together.

LAURENCE PARENT

residents who served and died in the First World War. The memorial appears as a simple colonnaded Doric temple nestled in a grove of trees.

THE WALL

Even after World War I, World War II, and the Korean War, little was done to memorialize veterans in the Nation's capital. After the Vietnam War, things began to change. The war in Vietnam lasted longer than any other American war. Over 58,000 American Servicemen and women were killed or remain missing in action in the conflict. When the war ended a small but determined group of veterans organized as the Vietnam Veterans Memorial Fund. They lobbied Congress for something tangible to be erected in Washington to honor and remember their "brothers" and "sisters" who had served and died in the conflict.

Their efforts were successful, and when the evocative Vietnam Veterans Memorial was com-

pleted, it presented itself as a very different kind of memorial. Maya Ying Lin, the Memorial's designer, adhered to the criteria specified by the veterans: (1) that it be reflective and contemplative, (2) that it harmonize with its surroundings, (3) that it contain the names of all who died or remain missing, and (4) that it make no political statement.

The result was an elegant black granite wall sunken into the landscape with names of all those who had died or were missing inscribed in shimmering black granite. Frederick Hart's statue of three servicemen, Glenna Goodacre's Vietnam

Overleaf: The sweeping "Freedom Wall" at the World War II Memorial includes 4,000 gold stars. Each star commemorates 100 Americans of the more than 400,000 who were killed in the war. Photo by Eric Long.

The snow-covered statues at the Korean War Veterans Memorial reflect the hardships of serving half a world away. The conflict took a heavy toll. Over 2.5 million military and civilian deaths are believed to have resulted from the war. Of those, approximately 38,000 were United States military deaths. Returning home, many veterans were not recognized for their service. The Korean War became known as "the Forgotten War." With the Korean War Veterans Memorial this began to change.

Women's Memorial, and a plaque honoring those who died as a result of their service, were added later to address other sentiments and give context to the war, but "the Wall" remained the memorial's most powerful element, with its polished granite surface of names.

THE WAR HALF A WORLD AWAY

The popularity and power of the Vietnam Veterans Memorial opened the way for new memorials to veterans. The next to be built was the Korean War Veterans Memorial. It was dedicated on July 27, 1995, on the 42nd anniversary of the armistice that ended the conflict. One-and-a-half million American men and women served in the Korean War. The memorial recalls the effort of the United States and its United Nations allies to repel the invasion of the Republic of South Korea by communist forces from North Korea.

The designers and planners of the Korean War Veterans Memorial wanted something that would clearly describe the character of this war half a world away. The most prominent feature is a group of 19 stainless-steel statues depicting a squad on patrol. A black granite wall with over two thousand sandblasted photographs of soldiers, sailors, airmen, and marines serves as backdrop to this dramatic tableau.

All the elements lead toward a reflective ceremonial "pool of remembrance." The defining inscription in the memorial reads, "Our Nation honors her sons and daughters who answered the call to defend a country they never knew and a people they never met."

·REVOLUTIONARY·WAR·1775-1783· *FRENCH·NAVAL·WAR·1798-1801* *TRIPOLI·1801-1805* *WAR·OF·1812-1815* *FLORIDA·INDIAN·WARS·1835-1842* *MEXIC*

ERIC LONG

The U.S. Marine Corps War Memorial is located adjacent to Arlington National Cemetery in Virginia and was based on a Pulitzer Prize winning photo taken by Joe Rosenthal on February 23, 1945 on the island of Iwo Jima. It depicts Marines raising the American flag on Mount Suribachi after enduring days of furious battle. Sculptor Felix de Weldon conducted a search for his subjects, but he could not locate some of them. They had been killed in action shortly after the famous photo was taken. The "Iwo Jima Memorial" honors all Marines who served since 1775. Encircling the statue's base are the names of wars and major campaigns recalling the numerous times in history when Marines served, fought and died for their country.

ANNE TUBIOLO

Sculptor Frederick Hart's evocative "Three Servicemen Statue" puts a human face on those who served in Vietnam. The bronze statue is realistic in many details, from the weapons they carry to the distant looks on the soldiers' youthful faces. In the sculptor's words, "Their strength and their vulnerability are both evident."

ERIC LONG

Sculptor Glenna Goodacre's Vietnam
Women's Memorial honors the thousands
of women who courageously served
"behind the lines" in Vietnam.

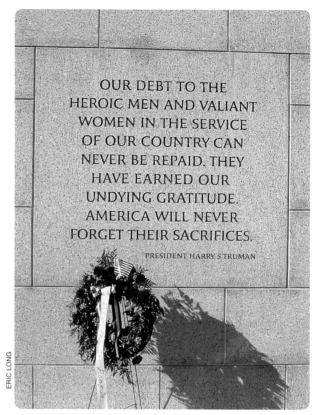

OUR DEBT TO THE
HEROIC MEN AND VALIANT
WOMEN IN THE SERVICE
OF OUR COUNTRY CAN
NEVER BE REPAID. THEY
HAVE EARNED OUR
UNDYING GRATITUDE.
AMERICA WILL NEVER
FORGET THEIR SACRIFICES.

PRESIDENT HARRY S TRUMAN

ERIC LONG

At *World War II's conclusion, President*
Harry Truman thanked those who sacrificed
for their country.

A DEFINING MOMENT

The sheer immensity of World War II called for something grand in the way of a memorial, and the site selected by the planners could not have been more prominent, a site directly between the Lincoln Memorial and the Washington Monument on the Mall. Opponents of the memorial site pointed out the historic uses of this location and the unobstructed view of the Mall it provided. The proponents of the plan pointed out that prominence was the point. World War II was the most cataclysmic event of the twentieth century, and the most devastating war in world history. The ferocity and scale of World War II affected every American. To the site's advocates, the memorial needed to be on a par with the greatest memorials in Washington. Ultimately they prevailed, and the expansive memorial was dedicated on May 29, 2004.

The World War II Memorial remains today as a tribute to the over 400,000 Americans who died in the conflict, the over 16 million who served, and the countless men and women on the homefront who worked and sacrificed to support the troops. Much of the dramatic view between the Lincoln Memorial and the Washington Monument was preserved in Friedrich St.Florian's final design. Two granite pavilions representing two theaters of war are set back from the viewshed accenting the setting; one represents the Pacific and the other the Atlantic. Pillars with bronze oak and wheat wreaths encircle the central ceremonial fountain. On each side of the memorial's entrance are 12 bas-relief sculptures in bronze recalling scenes of America at war. Taken as a whole, the memorial leaves no doubt that World War II was a defining moment for democracy and a defining moment for the world.

SUGGESTED READINGS

BRINKLEY, DOUGLAS, *The World War II Memorial: A Grateful Nation Remembers*, Harper Collins Publications, 2005.

HIGHSMITH, CAROL M., *Forgotten No More*, Chelsea Publishing Inc., and KWVM Production, Inc., 1995.

***T**he global and local nature of World War II is symbolized throughout the Memorial. Two pavilions* symbolize how the war was fought across two hemispheric zones – the Atlantic and Pacific. The fountains in front of the pavilions are inscribed with the names of corresponding key battles. Pillars represent states, territories, and the District of Columbia. Bronze wreaths of oak and wheat recall how industry and agriculture sustained the war effort. Everywhere are symbols and inscriptions reminding visitors of the scale and significance of this time when the world was at war.*

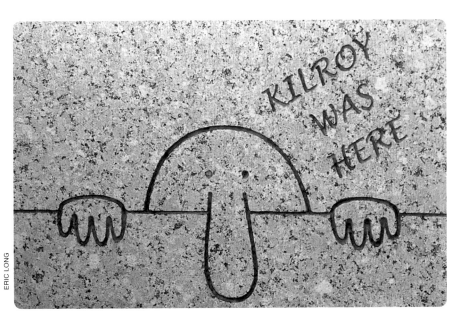

***"K**ilroy" became a craze during World War II. Soldiers left his image* everywhere, perhaps as an antidote to their stresses. Kilroy was there, and is inconspicuously included in the memorial.*

*It was one of the greatest stories
of his life that he was
not able to stand by himself,
but was able to get America back on its feet.*

Presidential Sites

Americans have taken their time when creating national memorials to presidents. George Washington was dead for 85 years before his monument was completed, Abraham Lincoln for 57, Franklin D. Roosevelt for 52, and Thomas Jefferson for well over a century. There has always been a healthy reluctance in the United States to create a national shrine to any one person, because there is no substitute for time when assessing enduring significance and meaning. The presidential memorials in Washington transcend personality and politics and continue to meet the test of time.

At the FDR Memorial the President's famous dog is memorialized. "Fala" went everywhere with the President, and now sits at his feet sculpted in bronze.

THE KNOW NOTHINGS

In 1791 when Pierre Charles L'Enfant mapped the city, he essentially established the basis for future parks and monuments. At what was then the western end of the Mall, and in line with both the White House and the U.S. Capitol, he called for a monument to President Washington. In 1833 a civic movement began that formed the Washington National Monument Society. The Society initiated a competition for an architect to build a monument to the First President. Architect Robert Mills, friend of Thomas Jefferson, was selected. He envisioned an obelisk surrounded by a Greek temple, with statues of prominent Americans, and a toga-clad Washington driving a chariot. In 1848 work started and progressed. In 1854 construction stopped at the 154-foot level of the obelisk as a result of the "Know Nothings."

The Know Nothings were a secret organization closely associated with a rising political movement called the American Party. When people asked about their activities members would respond, "I know nothing." In the 1850s the Know Nothings frequently engaged in hostile acts against immigrants, Catholics, and blacks. Hearing that the Vatican had donated a commemorative stone, Know Nothings raided the Washington Monument grounds, stole the stone, and destroyed it. Immediately afterwards the agitators took control of the

*T*he majestic Washington Monument stands out like the achievements of its namesake. However, it once stood unfinished and was lampooned and described as an eyesore. Today a faint change in stone color, partway up the obelisk, defines this period when it stood forsaken.

LAURENCE PARENT

Washington National Monument Society. What had been a patriotic national effort by citizens to raise funds from all Americans suddenly became politicized and radicalized.

The tumult of the times continued. Issues of slavery and states rights boiled over into a civil war. Construction of the monument came to a complete halt. During the war soldiers left graffiti on the unfinished structure's walls, and the grounds at the base of the monument, where the colonnaded temple had been envisioned, was fenced in and used as a stockyard and slaughterhouse. Even after peace returned the monument remained "a stump." Forlorn and unfinished, it was a sad reminder of the state of the Union.

> "Nothing more than the tallest chimney in the world, and perhaps the ugliest, which has nothing American in its character – nothing indicating it to be a monument to George Washington."
>
> W.W. STOREY TO WILLIAM CORCORAN 1878

A MONUMENTAL ACHIEVEMENT

Dramatic changes were in store for the Washington Monument following the American Centennial of Independence in 1876. President Grant provided for money to complete the obelisk, and the Washington National Monument Society ceded the site and construction to the government. Construction resumed under the supervision of Lieutenant Colonel Thomas Casey of the U.S. Army Corps of Engineers. Plans for the busy colonnaded temple at the base of the monument were abandoned; and a more classical, unadorned, dramatic obelisk took shape. On December 6, 1884 the 3,300-pound capstone was finally set in place at the top. The soaring 555-foot and 5-1/8-inch high memorial to America's first president stood as the tallest man-made structure in the world. Today the Washington Monument remains the tallest freestanding masonry structure. Spectacular and timeless, it soars high above the city, a testament to patriotism and vision. Still, to an observant eye, a slight color change in the monument's stone at the 150-foot level marks a time when both the monument, and a united America, were held hostage.

> "Taken by itself, the Washington Monument stands not only as one of the most stupendous works of man, but also as one of the most beautiful of human creations. Indeed, it is at once so great and so simple that it seems to be almost a work of nature."
>
> FREDRICK LAW OLMSTED

NS SO DEDICATED C

RE · WE ARE MET ON

EFIELD OF THAT WAR ·

TO DEDICATE A PORT

FIELD AS A FINAL R

FOR THOSE WHO HE

LIVES THAT THAT

LIVE · IT IS ALTOGET

AND PROPER THAT WE

HIS · BUT IN A LARGE

N NOT DEDICATE~WE C

ECRATE~WE CAN NOT

ROUND · THE BRAVE

D DEAD WHO STRUGG

CONSECRATED IT FA

OR POWER TO ADD OR

ORLD WILL LITTLE N

REMEMBER WH

JEFF GNASS

Although colossal in size, the statue of the *seated president appears intimate and lifelike. Lincoln looks comfortable but ready to stand. His hands are alternately at rest and clenched. His craggy features have a far away look, as if he is deep in thought.*

LINCOLN'S LEGACY

Two years after Lincoln's assassination, Congress called for a monument to honor his memory. Locating and selecting a design for the memorial proved to be a challenge and ideas were debated for years. In 1902 the McMillan Commission's idea to erect a memorial to the 16th President in an area where marshes existed was met with derision. Some questioned the practicality of constructing such a massive structure on fill drawn from the Potomac River. As the visual potential of this selected site became better understood, sentiments began to change. On Lincoln's 105th birthday, February 12, 1914, ground was broken for the Memorial in West Potomac Park.

The design for the Lincoln Memorial was chosen from a renowned architect, Henry Bacon. Bacon collaborated with sculptor Daniel Chester French. French would create the structure's focal attraction, a gigantic statue carved from 28 blocks of white Georgia marble depicting a seated President Lincoln. On Memorial Day, May 30, 1922, over 50,000 people gathered at the memorial for its dedication.

Within the chamber of the Lincoln Memorial one *can see etched in stone Lincoln's Second Inaugural Address and his Gettysburg Address. Here are the words, "With malice toward none; with charity for all...," and "...the last full measure of devotion...," sentiments of timeless relevance.*

The audience was segregated according to race; the arrangement seemed to contradict the Memorial's messages of fraternity and emancipation. However, on the dais, with former President and Chief Justice William Howard Taft, Lincoln's oldest son Robert Lincoln, and the President of the United States Warren G. Harding, was the keynote speaker, an African American and president of Tuskegee Institute, Dr. Robert Moton. Dr. Moton reminded the audience that Lincoln stood for more than union. His was a legacy of hope and freedom.

THE EDIFICE TO DEMOCRACY

The Thomas Jefferson Memorial is a memorial as grand as any in the capital, and one that by geographic placement compliments L'Enfant's vision. The Memorial's designer, John Russell Pope, modeled the structure after the Roman Pantheon, an architectural wonder that the 3rd President greatly admired. Seeking what was in essence a patriotic project of hope during the Great Depression, Congress in 1934 established the Thomas Jefferson

FRED HIRSCHMANN

ANNE TUBIOLO

Memorial Commission. The Commission was tasked with the selection of a memorial location and design. Almost immediately there was opposition to the plans for the memorial and the selection process. Some thought Pope's design was too pompous and grand for a time of national economic crisis. Others felt constructing a parkway or library to honor Jefferson would be more practical and fitting. But not even the Great Depression of the 1930s could stop the construction, and the Commission with the enthusiastic support of President Franklin D. Roosevelt pressed on.

When it came time to dedicate the memorial on April 13, 1943 (the 200th anniversary of Jefferson's birth) the Nation had gone from an economic depression to involvement in a world war. FDR still saw in the Thomas Jefferson Memorial intrinsic symbolic value. As author of the Declaration of Independence, Jefferson was one of the Nation's foremost advocates for freedom and democracy. In 1943 democracy itself was in peril from the expansion of fascism. Addressing the 5,000 spectators assembled, and a radio audience of millions, FDR said, "Today, in the midst of a great war for freedom, we dedicate a shrine to freedom."

"And they believe rightly; for I have sworn upon the altar of God, eternal hostility against every form of tyranny over the mind of man."

THOMAS JEFFERSON
IN A LETTER TO DR. BENJAMIN RUSH DATED SEPTEMBER 23, 1800.

President Thomas Jefferson was a statesman, scientist, architect, inventor, philosopher, musician, signer of the Declaration of Independence and founder of the University of Virginia. He served under Washington as the Secretary of State, and later was elected President.

The centerpiece of the FDR Memorial is a larger-than-life-sized statue of the 32nd President. It shows Roosevelt during his third term. Many upon seeing it were disappointed that this image did not reflect his disability. So a second statue was added to the memorial. It depicts the President in his first term, more vigorous, and unmistakably disabled.

MARK GIBSON

A MONUMENTAL CHALLENGE

President Franklin D. Roosevelt led the Nation through the two greatest crises of the twentieth century, the Great Depression and World War II. The FDR Memorial is a tribute to the 32nd President of the United States, and a tribute to all those who met the challenges of that critical period of history. In 1955 the Franklin Delano Roosevelt Memorial Commission was established by Congress to erect a memorial to America's longest serving president. Locating and designing the memorial was an arduous process and required several design competitions. In 1978 a design by landscape architect Lawrence Halprin was chosen. His concept called for an expansive memorial covering 7.5 acres with four outdoor "rooms" containing alcoves, sculptures, carvings, plantings and fountains, each room recalling one of the President's four terms in office.

Controversy ensued when it was noted that the President's likeness in the memorial did not clearly show he was disabled. As president, FDR was disabled from polio and unable to stand without assistance. It was one of the great stories of his life that he was not able to stand by himself, but was able to get America back on its feet. Disabled activists planned a protest for the memorial's dedication ceremony. As the dedication date approached, President Bill Clinton urged Congress to pass an act to include a statue in the memorial depicting FDR using his wheelchair. Legislation was passed and signed in time for the scheduled protest to be canceled. In May of 1997 the memorial opened to the public south of the Tidal Basin. Today a life-sized bronze statue of FDR greets visitors at the entrance to the memorial; he is depicted looking strong and determined, sitting confidently in his wheelchair.

SUGGESTED READINGS

ALLEN, THOMAS B., *The Washington Monument: It Stands for All,* Discovery Books, 2000.

HALPRIN, LAWRENCE *The Franklin Delano Roosevelt Memorial,* Chronicle Books LLC, 1997.

NATIONAL PARK SERVICE, *Lincoln Memorial Handbook,* U.S. Government Printing Office, 1986.

In 1861 she found her calling
and devoted her life to relief work.
During the Civil War, Clara Barton
organized civic efforts
to distribute provisions.

People with A Cause

"We are all children of the same Country"
—GEORGE WASHINGTON

CHAMPION OF FREEDOM

Through monuments, parks, and historic sites it is possible to connect with great Americans. On a hill overlooking the capital city, in the Anacostia neighborhood of Washington, DC, is the home of one such great American, Frederick Douglass. As a slave Douglass had educated himself and risked his life to escape to freedom. After his escape he dedicated himself to the abolition of slavery and published a newspaper called *The North Star*. As a popular orator he delivered speeches throughout the United States north of the Mason Dixon Line. During the Civil War he was able to meet with President Lincoln to advocate for fair treatment of the 200,000 African Americans serving in the Union army. With Lincoln, Frederick Douglass found a sympathetic ear and soon African American soldiers began to receive equipment and supplies, promotions and better pay. In referring to President Lincoln, Douglass said, "In his company I was never in any way reminded of my humble origin, or of my

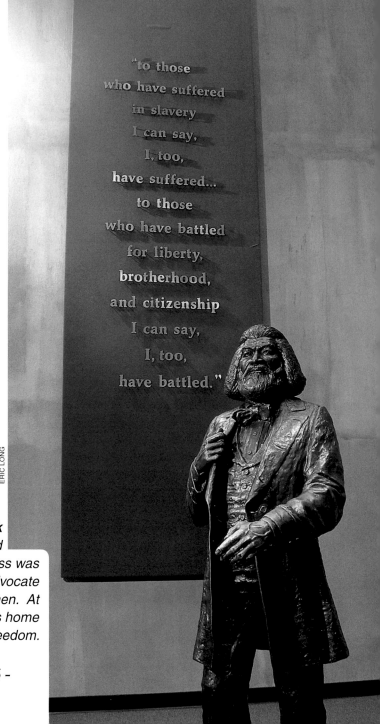

"to those who have suffered in slavery I can say, I, too, have suffered... to those who have battled for liberty, brotherhood, and citizenship I can say, I, too, have battled."

ERIC LONG

***S**lavery could not break the will and courage of Frederick Douglass. As a slave he made a harrowing escape and devoted the rest of his life to the cause of freedom. Douglass was constantly confronted by racism but persevered, not only to advocate for the rights of people of color, but also for the rights of women. At Frederick Douglass National Historic Site visitors can see his home and get up close to this champion of freedom.*

In 1891 two developers were so impressed by Clara Barton's *accomplishments that they built a large house and gave it to her. The spacious structure was located in the community of Glen Echo, Maryland. The practical Barton used the residence as a warehouse where she made space for herself, volunteers and staff. The building remained her home and office until she died at the age of 91 in 1912.*

ERIC LONG

unpopular color." Douglass and Lincoln continued to call on one another and became close associates. After President Lincoln's assassination, the president's wife, Mary Todd, took time to send Mr. Douglass the President's favorite walking stick.

Frederick Douglass continued his activism and worked with luminaries in the women's rights movement. He was appointed to numerous high government posts, including diplomatic positions in Haiti and the Dominican Republic.

In 1877 he purchased his home in Anacostia, a place he called "Cedar Hill." Here he wrote his autobiography and enjoyed an active family life. Frederick Douglass stayed active until the day he died. On February 20, 1895, at the age of 78, he had a fatal heart attack at home. He was enthusiastically telling his wife about a women's rights meeting he had attended earlier that day.

AN ANGEL OF MERCY

Until she was 39, there was little in Clara Barton's life that was extraordinary. She had taught in school, and worked as a clerk at the U.S. Patent Office in Washington, DC. In 1861 she found her calling and devoted her life to relief work. Responding to the needs of soldiers streaming into the capital during the early days of the Civil War, Barton organized civic efforts to distribute provisions. When she learned of the lack of supplies in army field hospitals, she organized groups of civilians who collected and distributed medical aid.

As the war continued, U.S. Surgeon General William Hammond granted her a general pass to travel with the Army Medical Corps. As she worked under horrible conditions, Barton won the admiration of many. Army Surgeon James Dunn wrote, "At a time when we were entirely out of dressings of every kind, she supplied us with everything, and while the shells were bursting in every direction... she staid dealing out shirts...and preparing soup... [She] was the angel of the battlefield."

As the war concluded, Barton worked to collect lists of dead and missing soldiers, and published the information in newspapers so that their families might learn of their fate. After traveling to Europe

and working with the International Red Cross, she returned to lobby Congress to establish an American Red Cross. Her efforts were successful and she became the organization's first president. Under her leadership the membership of the Red Cross grew rapidly and soon victims of fires, earthquakes, drought, tornados, hurricanes, floods, and epidemics were receiving assistance.

Today, as evidence of her single-minded devotion to relief work, one can tour her home in Glen Echo, Maryland. There, instead of trappings of domestic life, one sees a home that in every sense was the headquarters of the American Red Cross. Visitors to the site get an intimate look at the world of Clara Barton, and learn how she saved countless lives, aided thousands of victims, and mobilized a nation to care.

NPS PHOTO BY TERRY ADAMS

Mary McLeod Bethune is honored in Lincoln Park, one mile east of the U.S. Capitol. She was an educator, humanitarian and advisor to presidents. In 1935 she founded the National Association of Negro Women. The statue depicts her handing her legacy over to children. The National Park Service maintains Lincoln Park as well as her former home in northwest Washington.

ERIC LONG

Calm waters belie the fact that near the C&O Canal the Potomac River drops 75 feet in a half mile through a narrow gorge. The canal system is a remarkable engineering achievement and opened the way for river traffic and trade to points west. But even in 1828, as President John Quincy Adams was breaking ground for the canal, the B&O Railroad was being launched. Soon rail traffic eclipsed barge traffic and the canal, for a time, faded into obscurity.

A Supreme Effort

After the Second World War some members of the U.S. Congress expressed interest in turning the remainder of the C&O Canal that was not under the protection of the National Park Service into a parkway and commuter route. The fiercely independent, and sometimes controversial, U.S. Supreme Court Justice William O. Douglas, would have none of it. This "paving" of nature and history did not sit well with the avid hiker and outdoorsman.

Justice Douglas initiated a personal campaign to preserve the natural beauty of what had become a de facto natural preserve and pathway to history. He spoke frequently and passionately about the canal as a serpentine sanctuary, and led a campaign to save it.

Justice Douglas's efforts in 1954 culminated in a highly publicized eight-day hike where he challenged conservationists and news media to walk with him down the 184-mile-long canal from Cumberland, Maryland to Washington, DC.

It is estimated that over 50,000 people cheered on the intrepid hikers as they made their way to Washington. On the last night of the historic hike, Justice Douglas organized a committee that later made plans and recommendations to preserve the canal.

His efforts were successful; and in January 1971, President Richard Nixon signed the Chesapeake and Ohio Canal National Historical Park into law. The countless people who enjoy the Canal today can thank the tenacious and unorthodox Justice Douglas, who, when it came time to save this national treasure, put on his hiking boots and followed a path to success.

A Dream

The story of America is often a story of struggle. Whether it is a struggle for justice, peace, equal rights, or freedom it is often played out on the National Mall in view of national symbols and the halls of government. Here, gatherings and demonstrations sometimes number in the tens-of-thousands. In many respects they are living embodiments of a free nation.

"The struggle of today, is not altogether for today—
it is for a vast future also. With a reliance on
Providence, all the more firm and earnest, let us proceed
in the great task which events have devolved upon us."

—Abraham Lincoln

BOB ADELMAN / MAGNUM PHOTOS

***Dr.** Martin Luther King Jr.'s electrifying*
speech on August 28, 1963 from the steps of the
Lincoln Memorial is characterized as one of the
most inspirational moments in American history.
Surrounding him at the lectern were event organizers,
civil rights leaders as well as two representatives
of the National Park Service wearing their Stetsons.

One of the most celebrated events on the National Mall was the 1963 "March on Washington for Jobs and Freedom," when the Reverend Dr. Martin Luther King Jr. delivered a speech that galvanized the civil rights movement, and inspired people across the Nation. It was the 100th anniversary of Lincoln's Emancipation Proclamation, and over 250,000 people assembled at the Lincoln Memorial to hear speakers.

Dr. King was the last on the program. While in his speech he left his prepared text and looked up and began speaking from his heart. It came to be known as the "I Have a Dream Speech." His moving call for an end to racial prejudice and a rededication to the promise of the Nation, was broadcast nationally and became one of the most quoted public addresses of the 20th century. Today those visiting the Lincoln Memorial may well relive "the dream," as they stand where Dr. King stood, looking out over a vista of hope that is the Nation's capital.

> *"I often reflect that an American citizen cannot do a better thing for himself or for his country than to visit Washington at least once in his lifetime."*
>
> —FREDERICK DOUGLASS

ERIC LONG

The Old Post Office Tower rises 315 feet above Pennsylvania Avenue and offers spectacular views of the Capital. For many years some considered its Romanesque architecture outdated and out of place. In 1928 it was slated to be demolished, but preservationists prevailed and the building was saved. The old structure that once was derided as "the Old Tooth" is now considered a national treasure.

ERIC LONG

An unsuspecting hiker on Theodore Roosevelt Island may be surprised to find a national memorial on a trail. Nestled in a grove of trees is a grand statue of President Theodore Roosevelt with two ornamental fountains and four stone monoliths with etched Roosevelt quotes. To the planners of the memorial this 91-acre island in the Potomac, with its wetlands, walkways and wooded trails, provided the perfect setting, as President Roosevelt was one of America's foremost advocates for conservation.

The National Park areas of Washington DC are managed by the National Park Service. They include hundreds of individual sites visited annually by millions. They include historic buildings and archeological sites, as well as scenic drives, performance venues, and natural areas. They help protect the Chesapeake Bay watershed, and diverse plant and animal communities, including threatened and endangered species.

The monuments and the memorials in Washington are among the most spectacular and revered in the Nation. Biking, hiking, picnicking, performing arts, camping, horseback riding, and a wide range of sports activities are all available at the National Park areas in Washington. Even the White House buildings, grounds, and visitor information facilities are under the care of the National Park Service. Together, these places make the city a green oasis, and a world-renowned attraction.

Today many challenges exist for these National Park areas brought on by urban growth, pollution, heavy traffic, high visitation, and security concerns. Staff, volunteers, park partners and other stakeholders work diligently to protect these natural, cultural and recreational treasures. But if they are to survive and bring meaning to future generations, they must be understood without exception. You can protect the National Park areas in Washington, DC by getting to know them. Discover for yourself their significance - how they define America and give Americans hope.

MARK GIBSON

In 1882 an Anacostia resident planted some water lilies from his former home in Maine and started what was to become a wetland oasis. Kenilworth Aquatic Gardens, with its ponds and marshes, now includes wetland plants from around the world and remains an important habitat for water dependent wildlife.

ERIC LONG

The National Park Service's Mather Training Center is located in the historic town of Harpers Ferry, nestled in the West Virginia foothills about 70 miles northwest of Washington, DC. This facility for many years has prepared NPS employees in critical skills needed to serve the public and protect parklands.

NPS PHOTO BY TERRY ADAMS

Wolf Trap National Park for the Performing Arts became America's first National Park for the performing arts in 1966. Through a cooperative agreement between the National Park Service and the Wolf Trap Foundation, world-class performances are regularly scheduled for audiences of up to 7,000 people.

ERIC LONG

The famous Japanese flowering cherry trees encircle the Tidal Basin and accent views of the White House. Scenery in the national parks of Washington, DC can be striking, and sometimes even breathtaking. This is no accident. It is a result of generations of planners, designers, artists, gardeners, engineers, maintenance workers, and armies of volunteers. These picturesque places are now national parks and preserved "by the people and for the people." They are parks that look to the past with an eye toward the future.

- 42 -

The grave of President Kennedy, with its eternal flame, is on a hill in Arlington National Cemetery. When preparations were being made to find a resting place for the assassinated president, his brother, Attorney General Robert Kennedy, along with Secretary of Defense Robert McNamara, visited the cemetery. While scouting the area they walked up the hill to Arlington House, where a National Park Service ranger remarked how President Kennedy had visited before and said that the view was so magnificent he "could stay forever." The search was over for the scouting party. Today Arlington House, the grave of President Kennedy, and that of Robert Kennedy, are all on this hill with its spectacular view.

MARK GIBSON

Bicyclists pedal by what is commonly known as "the Navy and Marine Memorial" on the George Washington Memorial Parkway. The parkway is a winding 7,000-acre green oasis with historic sites, gardens and pathways. It hugs the banks and bluffs of the Potomac River and gives park goers spectacular views of the Capital.

ERIC LONG

The annual Easter Egg Roll brings children to the White House lawn at President's Park, and smiles to young and old.

MARK GIBSON

SUGGESTED READINGS

ANGELIS, GINA DE, *It Happened in Washington, D.C.*, The Globe Pequot Press, 2004.

BLUESTONE, CAROL AND SUSAN ERWIN, *Washington, D.C. Guidebook for Kids*, Noodle Pr, 2003.

BROKAW, TOM, *The Greatest Generation*, Random House, 2004.

GALLAGHER, HUGH GREGORY, *FDR's Splendid Deception*, Vandamere Press, 1999.

KYTLE, ELIZABETH, *Home on the Canal*, John Hopkins University Press, 1996.

PRYOR, ELIZABETH BROWN, *Clara Barton: Professional Angel*, University of Pennsylvania Press, 1988.

VOSS, FREDERICK S., *Majestic in His Wrath: A Pictorial Life of Frederick Douglass*, Smithsonian Institution Press, 1995.

SUGGESTED WEB SITES

www.nps.gov/cherry/

www.nps.gov/wamo/experience/view.htm

www.nps.gov/choh/BoatRides/PublicBoatRides.html

NON-NATIONAL PARK SERVICE SITES

Arlington National Cemetery
Bureau of Engraving and Printing
Federal Bureau of Investigation (FBI)
John F. Kennedy Center for the Performing Arts
Library of Congress • Mount Vernon
National Air and Space Museum
National Gallery of Art
National Geographic Society Explorers Hall
National Museum of Natural History
National Museum of the American Indian
National Portrait Gallery
National Zoological Park
United States Capitol Building
United States Holocaust Memorial Museum
United States Navy Memorial Museum

All About the National Parks of Washington, D.C.

National Park Service Sites

Chesapeake & Ohio Canal
National Historical Park
C&O Canal NHP Headquarters
1850 Dual Highway, Suite 100
Hagerstown, MD 21740-6620
301-739-4200
http://www.nps.gov/choh

Great Falls Tavern
Great Falls, Maryland
C & O Canal

Ford's Theatre National Historic Site
511 Tenth Street NW
Washington, DC 20004
202-426-6924
http://www.nps.gov/foth

The Petersen House

George Washington Memorial
Parkway Headquarters
Turkey Run Park
McLean, VA 22101
703-289-2500
http://www.nps.gov/gwmp

Great Falls, Virginia
Glen Echo Park
Arlington House/Robert E. Lee Memorial
Theodore Roosevelt Island Park
Clara Barton Parkway
Clara Barton National Historic Site
United States Marine Corps War Memorial

National Capital Parks – East
1900 Anacostia Drive, SE
Washington, DC 20020-6722
202-690-5185
http://www.nps.gov/nace

Anacostia Park
Kenilworth Aquatic Gardens
Frederick Douglass National Historic Site
Mary McLeod Bethune Council House National
   Historic Site
Fort Washington Park
Greenbelt Park
Oxon Cove Park & Oxon Hill Farm

National Mall and Memorial Parks
900 Ohio Dr, SW
Washington, DC 20024-2000
202.426.6841
http://www.nps.gov/nama

Constitution Gardens
DC War Memorial
Fifty-Six Signers of the Declaration of
   Independence Memorial
Franklin Delano Roosevelt Memorial
George Mason Memorial
John Ericsson Memorial
John Paul Jones Memorial
Korean War Veterans Memorial
Lincoln Memorial
National Law Enforcement Officers Memorial
Old Post Office Tower
Pennsylvania Avenue National Historic Site
Samuel F. DuPont Memorial
The National Mall
Thomas Jefferson Memorial
U.S. Navy Memorial
Ulysses S. Grant Memorial
Vietnam Veterans Memorial
Washington Monument
East and West Potomac Parks
World War II Memorial

President's Park
1450 Pennsylvania Avenue, NW
Washington, DC 20230
202-208-1631
http://www.nps.gov/whho

The White House
Lafayette Square
The Ellipse

Rock Creek Park
3545 Williamsburg Lane, NW
Washington, DC 20008
202-895-6070
http://www.nps.gov/rocr

Old Stone House
Peirce Mill
Fort Stevens

Wolf Trap National Park for the Performing Arts
1551 Trap Rd
Vienna, VA 22182-1643
703-255-1800
http://www.nps.gov/wotr

The Washington D.C. Area, capital

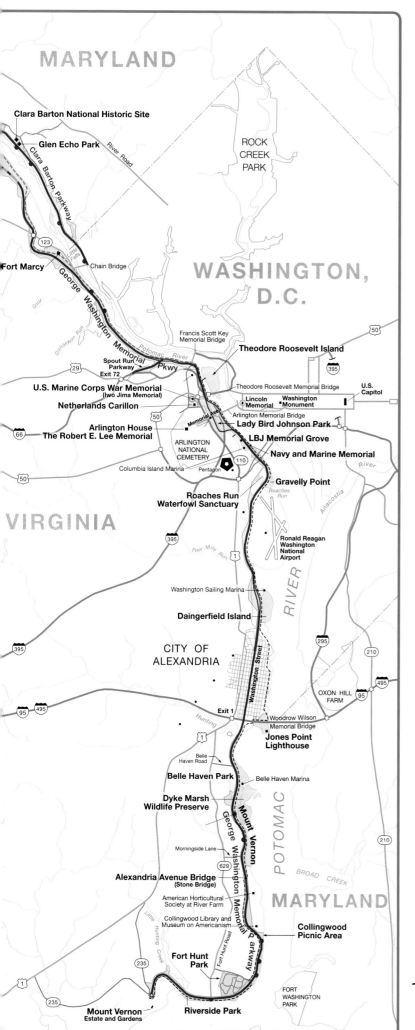

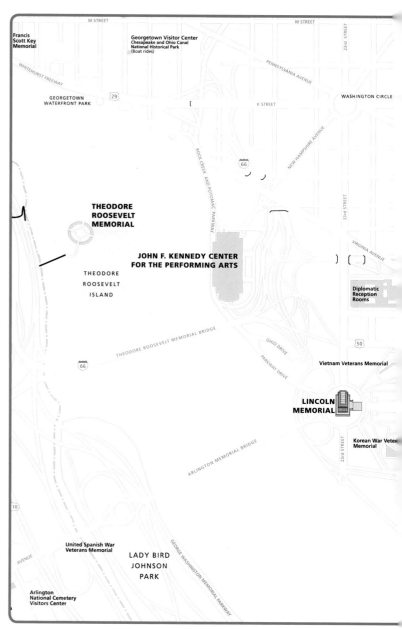

Looking at maps of Washington, DC one cannot help but notice it as a city of parks. The political nature of this vast federal enclave may be its greatest claim to fame, but politics aside, the scale and significance of its parks gives the city unrivaled distinction, and widespread allure and meaning.

The heart of the federal capital is an inviting open mall of green accented with monuments and memorials. Along the Potomac River is another park area, but this meandering stretch conforms more to the artistic preferences of nature. The George Washington Memorial Parkway begins south of Great Falls and winds along the banks of

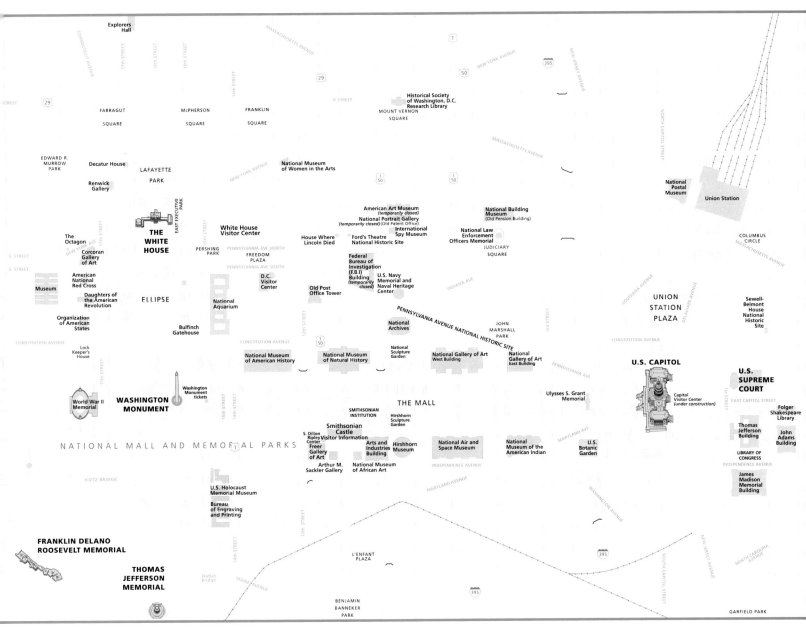

The following labels appear on the map:

Explorers Hall

Historical Society of Washington, D.C. Research Library

National Postal Museum

Union Station

FARRAGUT SQUARE

McPHERSON SQUARE

FRANKLIN SQUARE

MOUNT VERNON SQUARE

EDWARD R. MURROW PARK

Decatur House

LAFAYETTE PARK

National Museum of Women in the Arts

National Building Museum (Old Pension Building)

COLUMBUS CIRCLE

Renwick Gallery

EAST EXECUTIVE PARK

White House Visitor Center

American Art Museum (temporarily closed)
National Portrait Gallery (temporarily closed) (Old Patent Office)

National Law Enforcement Officers Memorial

The Octagon

Corcoran Gallery of Art

THE WHITE HOUSE

PERSHING PARK

House Where Lincoln Died

Ford's Theatre National Historic Site

International Spy Museum

JUDICIARY SQUARE

UNION STATION PLAZA

Sewell-Belmont House National Historic Site

FREEDOM PLAZA

PENNSYLVANIA AVE NORTH
PENNSYLVANIA AVE SOUTH

Federal Bureau of Investigation (F.B.I) Building (temporarily closed)

U.S. Navy Memorial and Naval Heritage Center

American National Red Cross

D.C. Visitor Center

Old Post Office Tower

Museum

Daughters of the American Revolution

ELLIPSE

National Aquarium

Organization of American States

Bulfinch Gatehouse

National Archives

JOHN MARSHALL PARK

PENNSYLVANIA AVENUE NATIONAL HISTORIC SITE

U.S. CAPITOL

U.S. SUPREME COURT

Lock Keeper's House

CONSTITUTION AVENUE

CONSTITUTION AVENUE

National Sculpture Garden

National Gallery of Art West Building

National Gallery of Art East Building

CONSTITUTION AVENUE

Capitol Visitor Center (under construction)

Folger Shakespeare Library

World War II Memorial

WASHINGTON MONUMENT

Washington Monument tickets

National Museum of American History

National Museum of Natural History

THE MALL

Ulysses S. Grant Memorial

Thomas Jefferson Building

John Adams Building

NATIONAL MALL AND MEMORIAL PARKS

SMITHSONIAN INSTITUTION

Hirshhorn Sculpture Garden

LIBRARY OF CONGRESS

Smithsonian Castle

S. Dillon Ripley Visitor Information Center

Freer Gallery of Art

Arts and Industries Building

Hirshhorn Museum

National Air and Space Museum

National Museum of the American Indian

U.S. Botanic Garden

James Madison Memorial Building

KUTZ BRIDGE

Arthur M. Sackler Gallery

National Museum of African Art

INDEPENDENCE AVENUE

INDEPENDENCE AVENUE

U.S. Holocaust Memorial Museum

Bureau of Engraving and Printing

FRANKLIN DELANO ROOSEVELT MEMORIAL

L'ENFANT PLAZA

THOMAS JEFFERSON MEMORIAL

Outlet Bridge

BENJAMIN BANNEKER PARK

GARFIELD PARK

the river passing historic sites, scenic overlooks, woodlands and gardens until it terminates at Mount Vernon, the long-time home of George Washington. The Clara Barton Parkway, the C & O Canal, and Rock Creek Parkway also dip into the capital, giving tourists and residents outstanding opportunities for exploration and enrichment. South of the Mall is National Capital Parks-East. Here are historic sites such as Frederick Douglass's home and Fort Washington, along with natural sanctuaries such as Kenilworth Aquatic Gardens. Wherever one goes in Washington they are not far from a National Park area.

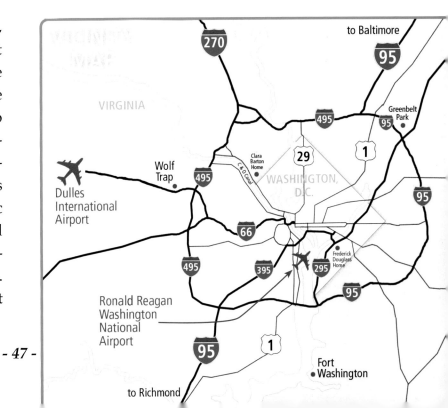

to Baltimore

270

95

VIRGINIA

495

Greenbelt Park

95

Clara Barton Home

29

1

Wolf Trap

495

C & O Canal

WASHINGTON, D.C.

Dulles International Airport

66

95

Frederick Douglass Home

495

395

295

95

Ronald Reagan Washington National Airport

Fort Washington

95

1

to Richmond

To the Future

What Pierre L'Enfant started in 1791 continues today. Growth and change in the National Parks of Washington DC will always reflect growth and change happening in America. Most recently, the National Mall and Memorial Parks Centennial Initiative has been launched. This revitalization effort coincides with the 100th anniversary of the National Park Service in 2016. Areas are being rehabilitated and designed to accommodate and engage new interests, needs and values; and new places are being considered for future preservation and public access.

Whatever tomorrow brings, at Great Falls people will continue to hear the roar of the rapids of an ancient river. At the Vietnam Veterans Memorial they will remember the sacrifice made by tens of thousands. At the Lincoln Memorial they will reflect upon the nation's legacy of freedom and struggle. At the homes of Frederick Douglass and Clara Barton they will discover the importance of standing up for principle and the potential of one person to make a difference.

Washington, DC will continue to be a place of parks, monuments and memorials, all of which are integral to the life of the nation and to the aspirations of the future.

FRED HIRSCHMANN

The White House is the temporary home of presidents, but a permanent home for an American idea. Each day park rangers welcome visitors from around the world to the White House. In doing so they open doors to history and help reveal an American legacy.

KC Publications has been the leading publisher of colorful, interpretive books about National Park areas, public lands, Indian lands, and related subjects for over 45 years. We have 5 active series—over 125 titles—with Translation Packages in up to 8 languages for over half the areas we cover. Write, call, or visit our web site for our full-color catalog.

Our series are:

The Story Behind the Scenery® – Compelling stories of over 65 National Park areas and similar Public Land areas. Some with Translation Packages.

in pictures... Nature's Continuing Story®– A companion, pictorially oriented, series on America's National Parks. All titles have Translation Packages.

For Young Adventurers® – Dedicated to young seekers and keepers of all things wild and sacred. Explore America's Heritage from A to Z.

Voyage of Discovery® – Exploration of the expansion of the western United States.

Indian Culture and the Southwest – All about Native Americans, past and present.

To receive our full-color catalog featuring over 125 titles—Books and other related specialty products:
Call (800) 626-9673, fax (928) 684-5189, write to the address below, or visit our web sites at www.kcpublications.com

Published by KC Publications, P.O. Box 3615, Wickenburg, AZ 85358

Created, Designed, and Published in the U.S.A.
Printed by Tien Wah Press (Pte.) Ltd, Singapore
Color Separations by United Graphic Pte. Ltd